SUSAN BLANSHARD

I0167698

SEND THE RAVEN

POEMS

PAGE ADDIE PRESS
UNITED KINGDOM

CONTENTS

Crows And Ravens	9
Translated	11
The Soothsayer	12
On The Grange	14
Paradise	16
Salvos	18
Small Mercies	20
The Epilogue	21
Khan's House	22
Stray Dog	24
Proxy	25
One Summer	27
Another Mirror	29
As Beauty Goes	30
About Sunset	32
Modern Plague	33
The Snow Angel	34
Grace For Twins	35
Crossing The Line	37
A Fragment	38
Behavior Of Luck	40
For Rossetti	41
Ecco Homo	42
Jewel Light	43
Auguries	44

The Living Past   46
Venetian Hours   47
The Leavers   48
The Eve   50
The Gypsies   51
Blessing The Spear   52
Angel In The House   53
The Mandate   55
The Doorkeeper   56
The Pearl Spoon   57
In Absence   58
Memorandum   59
Mortimer   61
Hours Of Thought   62
After Festus   63
On The Journey   64
The Writer's Song   65
Once In London   66
Postscript   67
Suffice   69
Dark Companion   70
The Sleeper   71
At Bridgewater   72
Impeachment   73
Night   74
At The Mews   75
Plague List   77
Sequel   79
Underwood   81

After Thought   83
Fire Song   85
One Day   86
The Alchemist   87
For Trudy   88
Fire And Snow   90
At Trial Bay   91
Endeavor   93
One Blue Moon   95
Travels In Antarctica   97
Anon   99
Opium   100
The Village Year   101
Companion Of Solitude   103
Old Movies   105
On Common Land   109
Silver Spoon   110
The Mill-House   111
Candle In The Mirror   112
The Desert   113
Diary Of Lost Man   115
The Late Salesman   117
Confession   118
Alveston Manor   119
Give Or Take   120
Stratford-Upon-Avon   123
Hallow Hall   125
Black Book   126
Quieter Histories   127

The City	129
The Room	130
The Signature	131
Traces	134
Prelude	135
Litmus	136
The Culvert	137
Epic Of Mind	138
If Astrid	140
For Maria	141
Compared	143
Twenty-First Century	145
The Envoi	147

'The innocent and the beautiful
Have no enemy but time'

—*W.B Yeats*

CROWS AND RAVENS

At the end of the hundred-year flood
some one will send the raven—

it turned out, daring after all,
often that crow or raven
re-appeared maleficent
and out of the dark, *unmoved*

brings a crowd of dead-ringers
dressed in black, untamed as flies,
watch them steal fortune away,
all those, whose words *spray out*

then vanish, like shapes that float
each precipice, its dark *loosed out,*
rattles awkward in the throat
ruin's raiment befalls families

when gifted thread is *blind cut*
one voice, for the raven cawing,
lamented, and the crows cawing
its best feather lost on the wing

one bird came to a branch of cedar
size of Jesus's cross, in case we forgot
the actual life—puts us here
I thought that I believed you
then all goes quiet—dark threat gone
as if nothing ever happened.

TRANSLATED

If I wore the same flower dress
would you remember the day?
garden of roses, bees in clover
and pressed the petals, yes
between summer's nakedness,
if I wore the same flower dress

we'll take Roman road back to our villa
clover, violet, and we grew nearer
hedonistic Elysium, white lilies
overgrown garden, the more it becomes
and as the hum of bees in ripening figs
and I, the same blue wedding dress

embroidered with figurative leaves
inclement images, itinerant bees
and it seems to me that things changed
no more in fifty years, when I heard
the sound of your voice, invisible things
we now are, what we bring—
here is some bread and honeycomb
here we are belonging again.

THE SOOTHSAYER

In another part of the world
they brew medicine for sadness
sugar floating with narcissus

they won't give her any
they say she is not a believer
in another part of the world

spring, summer, fall, winter
she spoke to me, as if I knew
numbers of luck and prosperity

in another part of the world
what collateral musters there
dries quicker than a single tear

now precious hallmark—raven,
engrave household silver for luck
for fortune, brings fortunes ill,

must the weak, become weaker still
twice cooked food, reconciled brother,

dying sister alone in ancestral house
but now, as the heart gives out
shall they hear—

        what never has been heard
through blind end of a stethoscope
sugar floating with narcissus
in another part of the world,

ON THE GRANGE

When I walk the snow land
The air is thick with shadows
As far as the eye could see
The fallen adventures before

Whenever dreams are real
When I walk the snow land
Home again in snowy fields
Knew the manifold of earth

As far as the eye could see
In the sudden quiet loneliness,
A fox appears amidst black sheep
When I walk the old land

Midnight in the shepherds' hour
They built castles in the stone walls
Twisting wattle for makeshift gates
Dry wood for roasting chestnuts

And the shepherd suddenly appears
The white moon with silence tonight
I want to speak— he is there to listen
Before a word is almost forgotten,

For richer or poorer, my bondage
Concur, familiar as hand in glove
When we walked the field of snow
And if it were true of anyone

You were the one gave the belonging
It is the white horizon-line
The heart of the winter all around us
As far as the eye could see—this longing.

PARADISE

On this island of the world
A wide veranda over a blue lagoon
I am passing the days in a hammock

Instead of a dirty corner alone
Suspicious, competitive, salacious
Hating the world of impossibilities

A wooden pier with deep water
Fishing strange fishes with spear—
Or hand-line, the barracuda

On this island of the world
From the depths of village tales
If they want to build a canoe

Take the sacred town axe
And each, their hunting knife
Eat a piece of roast pig for luck

If they want to build a canoe
Go out and drink coconut wine
And as they walk, they sing:

That is a tree, cut down the tree
We make a village boat
Heart-wood of the land

And when they find a large tree
All sit around it, and one by one,
Take turns to hollow the trunk

And shaping an out-rigger
And making the benches,
And wooden paddles

Go home and sing all night
For we have another canoe
Voice proud of the legend

Felled from the green jungle
The outrigger from a steeple of tree
Will bring in fish for the people
But when city men work together
They build a hotel casino.

Salvos

Lover, if I do not see you for a day
—I cannot sleep

only looking out for your return
but if never come back to me—
for the trouble with dreams

in tormented early hours
that imagine all things previous
the acuteness of what is remembered

for the trouble with itinerant dreams
that we would burn our house
to warm our hands, surrender all

a lustrous creed, lovely miracles
the silver riddle, chart-less talent
struggling with the multitude

but now, skin slips over worn bones
as death, like a covert, follows us—
ragged coat thrown around my shoulder

some say, woven *Cloak of the Old*
Cloak of the Wise, Cloak of a Child
if we grow older, but not very old
until—bones we donate to the earth
and clothes, to the Salvation Army.

SMALL MERCIES

Housed together, under one roof
because there is no other refuge
the darkness crossing your face

who is at fault, moving the pen
there was no miracle for us,
whoever signs the surname,

synonym for fate, kindling of universe
only a reflection, the mirror of a story
since all pen, paper, ink—delicate deed

haunted together, dispirited place
in merciless hands, receipts and fees
for everything is lost; to nothingness

if no one guards the treasure mine
we see again dreams extinction,
a great surge of fear , then loss

what if we live like the hero
ever know the fragmentation—
a spoonful of water makes a flood.

THE EPILOGUE

Cry the moment we are born
and every day shows why,
the honey is sweet but the bee stings

if filth rises under the white snow
if little is needed to make a sound
cry the moment we are born

if the cure is pills of cobwebs, sure
find ourselves old and out of blessings
the honey is sweet but the bee stings

and owing, more or less, of value
certain death's jest book, the origin
of the species, and vague probabilities,

the honey is sweet but the bee stings
what fear do we have, do you think
on a blue day like this—we are
poisoned by some secret grief.

KHAN'S HOUSE

Strange the tiger on parquet floor,
dead ears, amber glass eyes,
a dusty square of inanimate rug

it was easy to see it loitering
and has waited, came to life,
strange the tiger on parquet floor,

beloved of inanimate stealth
this, and a few other animals
a dusty square of innate rug

lay low, a collection of wild beasts
spiritless hunger and loss
choked the tiger, an end-day for him

by trigger's conviction, the hunted
The One, shot through the heart
ever since the bullets stoppage

a crowd of people, curs of the day,
and the eyes since then, so blindly
both torn, they could hardly see you

by way of timely preservation
add the power of killer-shaping
you see where claws spread

kept all its white bones, for luck
ivory teeth chipped on the upside
ever since the bullets havoc

the tail drags, like flag beyond repair
recounting a flayed struggle
the *Situation*, here and everywhere

yes, in this tameness, *Actual*
the hallway is reserved for entering
it is a ghost-animal who is there

under the comings and goings
lying about in the entrance hallway
even recounting such death-like use
says the *Master Auctioneer*—
it does beautifully, left as it is, *here*.

STRAY DOG

We return to the island by boat
Dogs are the first to recognize us
Heard the wisdom in a bark

One by one, the island dogs'
It is a stranger courage
A bark is the song of the dog

Beyond the throat, since starving
Poor animal returns empty-bellied,
From the Forest Monks' domain

It matters not what you like
But what likes you the best
A bark is the song of dog

Given me understanding
That it would leap from hell
Coming in with its shadow
It was true what you heard
That I called the black dog, home.

PROXY

It was the bare plain of your face
in the satin lined casket
the synthesis of suffering gone
silent, silent, silent, a trinity
no breath rises in you,
out of your hollow body

and would your eyes open
that gathered up your children
if I had that choice again
to say your name, would you see
beyond violet of the spectrum
you gave the very eyes of me—
                    softness of sage

they were your image and pain
the likes of you, laboring the silver
to set the table of wasting
you stirred the children's porridge
by your pale hand, in the kitchen
now every grey morning gone,

if I leave a letter in the casket
in silence, what is answerable?
there was a hardness of stone,
a mother's way of love,
chiseled from the heart,
all connected fragments
clue to the marrow—of mine.

ONE SUMMER

It's bright and early,
the wooded boats' rise up
wings or oars, who can tell
an expected change of swell

painted boats stay the jetty
it's bright and early,
as if anything can happen
lovers in a heart full rush

outside Florentine chapel
crossing the bridge of sighs
a luminous kiss, pose a photo
perfect in lovers' languages

we will go home by water
wings or oars, who can tell
past tangerine houses, tile roofs
laid out in afternoon sun

great door agape, chamber music
there are wedding rings engraved
gold against the honeyed sky,

you spoiled me, on the Ponte Vecchio
with you, around you, by you
the moment I undress in a hurry
all the while remembering
      —all lovely things returning.

ANOTHER MIRROR

Beauty worse than wine, intoxicating
who is this woman in the light?
her eyes so guard her foreign face
to gaze for the social repertoire
take a photo—for adult world

no human face is exactly the same
imperfection was a sign to be
her eyes so guard her face
perhaps, an ordinary woman
the lines on each side, part nascent

no perfection in its symmetry
in one look, a thousand mirrors
took a photo—in the adult world
her eyes so guard her face
pride is a smothering tribute

will she leave things as they are
nothing is rigidly perfect
the nature cannot be moved
but no one admits irregularity
Pheidias, sculpturing in snow
nothing but the chattering teeth
her eyes so guard her face.

AS BEAUTY GOES

He said that beauty was only relative
and with defect, what I asked was
what if you stay in full-bloom
unchanged, like a newborn proverb

further images on the social page
cuts a little more, like a bad scalpel
every smile, strangely done over
what if you stay in full bloom?
flashes of beauty came forwards

glimmer on the foolish side
further images on the social page
the expertness of primed needle
out to destroy expression for a while
—when a face will last forever

what if you stay in full bloom
more from mouths with gold-fish lips
some bee had a word, then stung it
and a new woman looked up

queen of bohemia, or inglorious angel
puts on perfection to last a while
pale colors of mineral make-up
dark kohl eyes, twice as earthy
the women as she wants to be

there was teasing, arguments and jealousy
never leaves her beautiful face, unmade
Internet trolls spied more narrowly
further images on the social page
found fault with the woman within.

About Sunset

There is music he played once
fifty years ago—she knows
yule-wood violin has one song
when the bow bends low,
when all sunflowers burn to husk
yule-wood violin has one song
send for the raven, if not, the crow
past feather fences in a row
when she looks back, she knows
there is music he played once
the red sun behind him, wilder
he seemed to be standing in fire
the rest of life beyond this day
rocks of spine belong to the past
and I, longing, alone, and lonely
if lovers' meet in distant mid-winter
do the eyes of a lover grow older?
do you recognize first, her face
or sound of her voice in the night-scape,
—perhaps, perhaps, perhaps.

MODERN PLAGUE

As plagues grippe tightens
the world's map in red
people are left estranged
from usual patterns,

a skeleton of regular life
has been picked clean
feeble feet outrun fever
virus hides in a sneeze,

a year of tremulous blackness
as army sleeps on marble floors
months drags on, precipitate loss
rampant with uncivil chaos

razor wire, fences and barriers
year of pandemic pandemonium
all flags lower than half-mast,
who can prophesy future
even after a world plague
—long black shadows follow.

THE SNOW ANGEL

When the pigeon seizes the sparrow's nest
it doesn't know, how to build its own
we take our separate memories

together in the garden of illusionary
as tear filled eyes, mimic rain's glass
our children, off like gypsy swallows,
passing already incognito,

practiced in the art of good-bye
then I turn, light in front of your face;
white like elderflower, pale as lily
all the troupes—in paper masks

when I turned back, your shadow
was in my place, lightly sorrowed
but if you ever go—my shadow will follow.

GRACE FOR TWINS

They entered the *City of Nowhere*
through the maze of the heart
Byron said one summer's day
happiness was born a twin

through the maze of the heart
when the wine flowed like a river
happiness was born a twin
and he kissed his lover, through mist

they entered the *City of Nowhere*
when the wine flowed like a river
and he kissed his lover
under the flowering peach

when the wine flowed like a river
there were the usual pleasures,
and he kissed his lover,
Byron said one summer's day

it takes two for a kiss
at all times they are together

no boundary would ever change
they entered the *City of Nowhere*

Byron said one summer's day.
wet the ink-stone, dip the pen
move into this place by music
to make a private requiem,

of which heart song—*One* belongs *Two*
as they entered the *City of Nowhere*
through the maze of the heart
towards which we only dream
and—dreams keep the dreamers, here.

CROSSING THE LINE

If you could read wet tea leaves
in the bottom of chivalrous cup
the bees attentive to the flowers
and if you knew more than before

and still, the dark patterns come
once the honey is done, time again
all wild places, pavilions of chaos
the bees attentive to the flowers

one day I came with you, to see
all the *horseshoers*, all the *do-gooders*,
all the *believers,* all the *receivers*
a little promise made with the debris

of those gold and marble palaces
all perfection vanquished to nothing
an illusion, with all its cresset
passe, the oak tree on solid rock
though bent a little more in cadence
every woman stands with the help of sadness
all the predictions that are true—
what high-life shall we return too?

A FRAGMENT

Dreams we bought for paper dollars
before ink dries on the title deed
the house begins to attach itself
to what we have, for what we are
the instant children, and espresso cups

as solid walls fold around us,
like two arms with certain snugness
house-shaped island, above the bay
moors to the family, each holiday
always going there in a thought

and the door locked without a key
perhaps, bright reverie, simple past
archway of acorn and blackberry briar
what way did we come? This far?

I hear sound of rain on roof
like impassion whisper within
each dusty closed forgotten room
knows our road-wearied tread
bamboo mat becomes feather bed

who will remember, what comes after?
suitcases thrust away into a corner
back with young daughter, to teach her
names of roses and wildflowers,
all that pretty the world
or sit by her bed when it thunders.

Behavior Of Luck

The moon darkens where I cross the river
The sun is about to set when I board the boat

If you wonder where she belongs—
Ever ask the seas, while swimming
Ever find the answer to the deep
In a river of sinking troubles

The net waits, with nothing in it
I remember all your words
Fragility becomes the heart of us
I have seen, and such a price,

No one should ever hear loss twice
The winner's shout, the loser's curse
The river has drowned the white horses
All the ways to hush up the truth
With rising oars, we kept our time
Damned dreamers in a sinking boat.

FOR ROSSETTI

A scribble of notes sent by messenger
to the annex of quarantine villa
silent virus spread like a nightmare,
until I wished to belong, elsewhere

the way it is; even a mosquito
fights over a drop of common blood
then I lay your envelope on the bed
from letter to letter, ramble like roses

show a pen rarely leaves the paper,
you write in cipher, but in French as well
and in this fever's distillery, some proof
even as the most scabrous perfume

astonishing as sultry neroli perfume
received by the wrist and nape, so it is
I only need a lover, not a doctor
kissing you in a time of plague,
like the Madonna of the Abandoned

            as you open the door
unmasked our beautiful quarantine.

Ecco Homo

A man appeared, in a class of animal
That had broken through, and escaped
His flaws untamed and lurking

As if man shaped inclement demons
Thoughts and maleficent intentions
He was all we could never be

All the world could never know
His flaws untamed and lurking
All that he deemed to say or do

Although unknown to—two
A man appeared, in a class of animal
Still, he held out his hand

Grief and vexation, a Jacobite curse
Cold grip sealed impoverishment
Brought down through centuries

To tease *The Watch Dog of Fate*—
The eyes of his, gave nothing human

We left, shaking hands the devil
Evil eye, to harass the mind,
Further trouble came by multitudes.

JEWEL LIGHT

There was a cache of gifts,
sapphire ring you gave me
cornflower blue, a thousand facets
right gift—at right time of year

in jeweled instance—beautiful
like a blue eye, a sound-less blink
and now, doubly reminisced
that somehow, disappears

there is an angel in greater house
love that is named, if I listen at the culvert
the memories magnetic troupe
magnifies in the jeweler's loupe
to remind me—I belonged most to you.

AUGURIES

Came back to see the old house—
with dreams of haunting this place
as if we were once, *The Owners*

feel the privilege to belong—still
curious, if nothing less galvanized
came back to see the old house—

dull rumors confuse the memory
they heard talk of grand error
careless deal of nonchalance

memory tricks the door open
we never moved from there
the more we found it, beautiful

countless prayer rugs, gardens
with peacocks and turtle doves,
lemons and oranges, gifts of Babylon
and the smell of toast and butter
this life, for *The Dream Watcher*

the memory will need no eyes
rosettes of roses engrave old wallpaper
the fireplace stoked dark-red embers
children's voices light-hearted,
                    saying something.

THE LIVING PAST

You and I are not yet old
what to give, when all is gone
but yet are nothing young

we have lived through
the fated forty-seven years
still, more was expected

remorse infused all things
our clothes, our hair, our eyes
even the words we speak

you and I are not yet old
how little we have gained
how vast the unattained

perhaps, destined pilgrims
you and I are not yet old—
but yet are nothing young
prostrate on the grass of sorrow
reproves us, like the comforter of Job.

VENETIAN HOURS

In a city of extraordinary light
a place to notice exquisite sights
in the room at any given moment,

bolts of angelic mid-day sun,
slant through verdigris shutters
to take a short-cut through the day

a passion-given look, for the lover,
wild, the honeyed body, your face,
this place with you, whose lips says

what has been warm all over
one place, one kiss, and then another,
last scene of all, this afternoon tryst

before I heard the taxi leaving,
for it would be, I, alone in Venice
left on the bridge, as only an ordinary tourist.
nothing is left to be, for what has been
                              —is gone.

THE LEAVERS

All memories are exhausted
we have reached our limits
left behind the mainstream

there is no blue room here,
we cannot make our way back
                    to the front gate
to help you down the stairs, again

the coffee in the cup gone cold
the familiar love and talk also
cornflower sapphire ring sold

doors are locked, shutters closed
in a swift cleft of dejection
the suicide chair, re-upholstered
amidst the clutter and cigarettes

final letter typed in a hurry
in the luminous garden
there is fruit cake in the oven
and an overbearing perfume

the hallway fills with laughter
with no voices it knows
all memories are exhausted
we have reached our limits
what are we doing back here?

THE EVE

I saw the day coming, the image
Formed on a far horizon
There is a child between us
A marriage, an artist's notebook
A diary filled with exquisite nights
Brambles beside pilgrims' path
Hedgerow berries for the wanderers
You and I finish the calvados—
Spirits and embers, how seasons knew,
Burning through the solitary winter
Here where you and I met
There is a child between us—
I see the undying place
Where the black bees whisper
Bearing all our dreams and wishes
Timeless like fleeting summer
Appearing on the horizon.

THE GYPSIES

The Keeper holds up a fistful of keys
through convict brick and gray ashes
the only one who loves and pities

what we gave, we have
what we spent, we had
what we left, we lost

Perhaps—*The Keeper* holds keys
to each house and every known garden
a delusion from naught to nothingness

what we gave, we have
what we spent, we had
what we left, we lost

when you have them,
they are not worth a lifetime
slip out the back, *The Keeper* said.

BLESSING THE SPEAR

If people should ask where I belong—
with you, traveler, at the world's end
two grains of sand, a wandering sound

you and I against enameled eye,
retrieves names, and prophesies
until our thoughts blistered

twenty-years artifice in old cities
reversal of luck, forlorn fortune cards
of eagle, hawk or dove, such pretense

the raven's cry means money coming
or predicts the state of kingdom
at the start, a silver pen and indigo

black curve, the arc of signature
there was a truth, red ink involved
written in the book, anonymous error

eddying dollars, or random misprint
as if, wrought only to us

every ink from every pen's fountain,
all the truth that the word invented
a sense of how not to cry.

ANGEL IN THE HOUSE

We spent a ludicrous year
in the province of miseries havoc
no one could tame the pandemic
they kept a corner for survival
in pathos of pandemonium
unrelated talk, became interesting
arguing politics with several Angels
critical of people's main chance
in these most dangerous days,
not safe from traps and snares,
at once we found ourselves
writing what was worth reading
painting was worth seeing
baking what we may devour
inside a grand mansion house
rich garden of peacock plumes

whatever we wished; we see
while others entrench in wards
and the vaccine, if it will ever be—
now, one by one, first sod, then grass
everything goes beyond, darkest earth
goes the sextants spade, by heavy load
possible to number the dead, all deadly
possible to number each grain of dirt
each drop of rain that falls from the sky
impossible to count drops of tears
that fell this year, from our eyes.

THE MANDATE

Living what was worth living
addicted to pleasure state
but then, a knock on the door,
an appearance before iron gate
obedient dog, tame-charm snake
when *The Gate Man* answers
the auspicious guest enters
but then, a knock on the door,
a nod of the head, salutation
refers question in their mind
living, what was worth living
all mansions, crumble and fall,
answer the wrecker ball, empty of all,
beyond the envy, and begin over
on a shoulder of another street
the yard mossy and overgrown
the neighbors talking in hushed tones
who will number the fallen stones.

THE DOORKEEPER

This house rose in his mind, unheralded

There is a white painted house
with views out over Soldier Bay
beyond that, old wooden wharf

kauri boats load sugar cane
warm shelter, someone's home
there is a white painted house

carved columns have grown
from colossal dream, in stone,
beyond that, old wooden wharf

return home, door's open wide
comfortable smell of toast inside;
makes itself felt, like sudden breath

there is a white painted house
beyond that, old wooden wharf
home is like an open wound—
if only they had fought to stay.

THE PEARL SPOON

The feast of Virgin and Martyr,
astronomically, fell on shortest day
a day of riddles and influence

nothing to eat but kinds of caviar
pale sturgeon roe, deep pearl spoon
the feast of Virgin and Martyr,

then came December's blue moon
the women of influence still
a day of riddles and influence

gifts or possessions, change her
and so on, diamond tennis bracelet
the feast of Virgin and Martyr,

neroli perfume, designer paper mask,
sixty-thousand-dollar crocodile bag, yet
refuse to hold the gift-giver's hand
if he is a player or rapist, or abuser
or out to use her—every woman knows.

In Absence

Wherever he goes, prodigal man
betrays his last hiding place,

completes the darkness, belabors
fate slips visceral vision;

forfeit the key, after all
what Devil destroys, writ the blood

a traveler is a stranger, by chance
no sooner every honest name is read

then the silence will deafen
crush the world like a great mirror
and shiver into a thousand pieces.

MEMORANDUM

Some place in the world
I lost a treasured thing
small as sparrow's egg
cast away, like ivory rune

though I meant to keep it
goes itself—a thousand places
I held up my hand for silence
as the sound of child fades

first came baby shoes,
rose bud shawl, fine wool
not since, a mother's cradle
even as death drawer falls open

since every woman is beautiful
now my hair, winter white
the features of faces, tarnish
pale green eyes, slumberous

not long after, opium pipe
draught smoke shows

a thousand peaceful dragon ways
to dream flame, its usual fire

there are fragments of the heart
slowly moving warm blood
engraved, embossed, embedded
now we come, now we go

vines of our fingers entwine,
heaven-felt hand in velvet glove
yet, even if, I turned, after
they take your hand away

one minute, or a year, left
everything that was, is less
when its over—and your eyes shut
but then, you wrap a scarf of red

age-worn, moth-holed, one
blood stain of your blood, one
transfusion of the lovers' heart
with you, and, with you
our blood types, archetypal
belonging has its purpose.

MORTIMER

Before I leave, shall I lay a handful
of roses on your grave,
if so, how many to be exact?
for a mathematician, is particular

A graveyard, immeasurable, she'd say
even the stone-roses in scripted mausoleum
begin to turn real—the angels' also
one or two precious women

She'd say well, I wasted life on a man
with a French accent, it was though
as passionate, as complicated
as individual, as bewildered rhyme

He spent two months over a poem
to describe the feelings of fish
a reason for bouillabaisse,
traditional and pelagic

L'Allegro, do you know?
it was the end of August
I thought you knew I knew you knew
it's late, good-night friend.

HOURS OF THOUGHT

Activists made a right turn,
a detour to Pennsylvania Avenue

board up luxe stores
before next riotous interval

extreme part of history, said
Exodus, Genesis, and Numbers

they set up a noise like bullets
tore down flags in a crush,

removed stars from the histories
reverence in the portrait gallery,

with blood on hands, broke doors
waved stripes off civil cloth
as lies came almost with truth
conjurers' and jesters' in a line
beginning in the Garden of Eden
ending in The White House rose garden.

AFTER FESTUS

In barbarous days, the worst ways
poisoned by shallow answers,
or what the world tells you,
the wrong wants righting
in the old days, the gage of yesterday
that no human had seen or heard
to know all is to forgive all.

ON THE JOURNEY

What of the child of December's night
that any passing love-child understood
as innocence enrolls the infant son

new arrival, draws first breath
as babe lays in manger's straw
what mattered more than the babies did

newborn to the sound of infinities,
baffled as we are, the self-same day,
the oasis shelters the wanderer

now the swaddled one gives up the cradle
runcible spoon turns silver, then gold
all mothers' are written in *The Book*
crib empty, wind breaks the branch
and all the while goes a-lilting —
musical boxes, a lullaby.

THE WRITER'S SONG

Today, as windows flung open
and all the bright sunlight—happens
more word of you, and in the book

indelible ink in the blackening
understanding every mistake,
makes one more forgiving

empty page draws own conclusion
the transforming thought, invisible,
yet goes on forever, like the gold rain

and the peacock of gold, in evergreen tree
this is what *The Author* shows us,
this, without misprint.

Once In London

In the pure severities of domesticity
and who were simply slaves

they climb up narrow chimneys
sweep aside an innocent generation

black wood, iron bark, the dark glass
children of mines and brick-fields

threatened with utter destruction
whiskey bottle, whip of willow

with bated breath, the impatience
bridge of sighs, song of laborer

song of shirt—cancel another out
to slightly vanish, out of sight
without a trace of permanence.

POSTSCRIPT

Captain brought up children
nodding, at a way of life,
stoke the embers on Sunday

No offspring of yours, begs to be
born, innocents fed honey, or lies
trapped like bees inside a glass hive

There is no place less darkling,
each child, on bee-line tumble
the heart will turn to marble

And rain fell as fine feathers
enough things found, cannot be
because we did not see them

Captain passes the bowl,
with soured milk and ashes,
as if a lesson given by a saint

As the children grow frightened
the stupid, insolents, who may
or may not, in any way disobey

It's like talking to disobedient dog,
a formal tone to beg or placate,
on the other side of despair,

And then by way of sharp dismissal
waste of precious, but then, refusal
lips fluttering like tired moths',
cold shallow bath in winter
poor excuses make rich punishment—
rather a ship than a family, he told her later.

SUFFICE

Someplace it happened
locked in, locked out
tamed with a conjurer's stick
the boot, hard slap, high kick
leather belt's protruded buckle
how the girl is broken
fistful of brutish knuckle
either way, fast makes bruise
draws the blood, thin bone crack
sometime it happened
how the boy is broken,
somewhere it happened

not tall enough, to leave the house
for, they cannot yet reach, the door handle.

DARK COMPANION

Out of the Dead's deceiving dark
that hides the stars, and magnifies the grass
is darkness too, a seal of redemption
or, distracted, some dark kindred
born of dusty bone, a high message
of secrets, the gravity belongs afterwards
what of the Darkness, how will—belonging
if the time will come around again,
ask the winter for summer, oak trees green
and childhood's lost swing, is found again.

THE SLEEPER

Heart-blood at winter's hearth
life is only a fraction of time,

outlearned and outlived
in spite of the need for breath

only to leave, when heart cease
a loud stunning silence,

as eyes fill with the purple
dark that shows sod so great,

and woman so small, the math
moreover, this vague disquiet

empty places count for nothing
when she is gone.

At Bridgewater

Thoughts of a double death, tragic
yesterday's ashes tipped in a hurry
down a soldier-ant nest, rotten branch
as if, simply putting out the garbage
why fill the hollow log with precious jewels—
a leaf will not return to a dead peach tree
even ants are confused—*why not wait?*

IMPEACHMENT

A sober unmasked man
stood out in a warbled crowd
all by the desire of the moth
for the star, for his strategy

to raise the black glove fist
a hand of violence, out of hell
that might grind down hearts
of men and women, who would tell

and who did know too well
listen to barrage of dug up lies
the half-truths by a land slide,
he drove by, marshalled by fame

now bones crack at his name
plagues the marrow of existence
cities no longer recognize each other
all by the desire of the troubled
                         for the stardom
children on the borderland, on their own
we did not ask for this—brazen imperfection.

Night

I heard enough of last night's wind
on the first pear blossoms
during a week of monsoon

now the whole courtyard, this hour
is filled with rhyme of wind-bells
nothing is left, except drip of rain

the sound of bamboo flute
locks emptiness in the room
the wind gnaws each inscription

yellow chrysanthemum bloom
only brother lost in the monsoon
all gold gathered up in iron net

we watched prosperity
we watched decline—
the rise and fall of houses
under the waning moon

near the house of landslide dragon
a line of white heron takes off.

At The Mews

A glass of water, a bowl of pears
she died alone in the room upstairs
Thorn Terrace, two up, two down
a little too far to walk into town

she lived on one pension, or another,
recipe for beet soup from her mother
bone-bolted hips, stiff, in pain's way;
death sat with her, an hour yesterday

asks in her gentile voice, mirrors of time,
how do you know when the heart gives out
how much to pay the perpetual gardener
sweet-pea tuberose tulip wallflower

prolific and profuse, perfume sublime
and butterfly alights on velveteen wings
but when the purse goes empty, tomorrow
who shall tame hedge and weeds of sorrow

hang the thorns and brambles on the trees
the garden haunted by funeral lilies

then she drew one deep breath,
it is unpredictable, to die alone

I begin to think, death overhears, more
even a gilt mirror opposite the door
gives no reflection of ill-fated agenda
one thing leads to another, one hour

the silence notes an undelivered breath
morning includes you, benighted in death
with an expression, alters your eyes
they are dark roses where rain pearls hide

even your face as it departs, has its smile
now your home is deceased estate
one in a row of painted doors, closed
like a half-hearted summer —goes

even cohort shadows wish to leave,
shut the doors after you go
your shoes left in the white hallway
left what was before you
and what was behind you
old house left —undeniably empty.

PLAGUE LIST

It is the second year of pandemic

memoirs tinged with mercies
give blood back to shadows
it seems this year is tumultuous
who is safe, are we really?

those who have too little or nothing
even out of nothingness, one breath
unless forgone, blasted by fever—
write grave list of casualties

from the greater plague histories
list of dead issued weekly
kill us all, one by one, death now
dead to all, lonely one, die now

during periods of pandemic
everyday life shrunk to its margin
the list as long as casualties
never give up on finding a vaccine

indebted for philosophers of hope
to live out these dark months—
in the winter of pandemic
every godforsaken needle,

petitions the gods', for us
there are lilies on new graves
glowing like pale wax,
in some perfectly transparent way—
as if flowers for the living.

SEQUEL

All the time I was younger
I did not know I was aging
all the time you were sick
I did not know you were dying

nothing but that—slipping away
feeling, held your hand
against my cheek, as if I
        could give it warmth,

night follows candle-mass
a stone-smile held my lips
in beautiful expression, as if—
angelic could kill a fever

catch us out for being ill
sad news, and likewise
the person who sent it
every word, a bitter pill

true-love knots into iron wreath
the mead of melodious tears

but then, sister of small mercies
runs her fingers, like a comb
through our silvered hair

but now, last breath—
dust and feathers do not lift
when I follow you seamless earth
simply into one narrow space
to lie beyond the quiet, where you are.

UNDERWOOD

Dangerous to live in a plague-filled world
in twenty thousand and twenty-one
all the luck we could muster to save us
crystal ball, rabbit foot, get-well word

the ones that could surmise fate
saw piles of significant bone dust,
such cruel years go sliding past
first one, then another, five years

white the cloth of mortality, we met
those who stop by to enshroud us
everyone masked and gowned
now, all remains, in plague years

Bruegelesque painting in the gallery
of the life before, the afterlife
lung full of precious breath
preserved like its own miracle

to suffer the blight of famine
in flesh and blood, we become

some revelation of world suffering
unbeaten, each exquisite heart
if all are gone, no human left—
who shall write this epitaph?

AFTER THOUGHT

The White House gives advantage
rose garden and office of oval
topiary cut to a Leader's gamble
duck pond filled with duckweed

everything breaks quiet solitude
while the wife wraps wedding china
in yesterday's national newspaper
pardon your son, pardon your daughter

like a queue of dusty shrines
in the center of the hot, dark hive
inside White House trompe-l'oeil
radiates from angels' hell venue

front door open, hand and glove
wilder hands and wilder fingers
or toss a little lie on paper, as well
write the defamation, before translation

after all summer parties end
evening clothes shut from daylight

who they are and have been?
this post-humus invitation
claustrophobic etiquette and manners
white gloves and calling cards
will not be left tomorrow.

FIRE SONG

Intrusion of rain on vacant stairs
one dog barks now and then
already making me nervous

dog caged up at midnight
watches the red against white
at the edge of sunken world

under a dying sun like blood
the ashes have blazed
ten thousand years, too long

on the verge, so many things
it's the moment that counts
rotten wood is unfit for burning

even a fire is lit by damp match
no one is there to ask for kindling
only a lone egret beside the tall grass,
we feed ourselves on the color of rice fields.

ONE DAY

Something that occurred to us
before the vaccine roll-out
first thought was to stay alive
summoned the gods of craft
to make a billion gloves
a million facial masks
checkered, floral, paisley
combinations of randomness
beyond the stockpiles
half a million dead in the cities
dark vial, of strangers' blood
test positive for the virus
makeshift morgues overflowing
the virus spread to New Guinea
everything changed—since you left
and here at grave's end
speed the gravestone's morose
inscription, in scrabbled creases
left by moss and stone,
an epitaph for a journey
and then you must start out
                  all over again
until the plague of plague vanished.

THE ALCHEMIST

I saw you cross, a woman's hand
With gold, turn back to see a painter
    and her cross-eyed son

I saw you make the gold
From poor-man's metal
—a pauper's transient formula,

Making gold from wheat
Cut a straw into fine nips
Put them in frozen water

Strain gold liquid, shallow dish
Leave it to stand for one day
Until pure gold surfaces,

Richer beyond poor, alchemy's error
Palace inhabited fools' wealth
Honey on the cliff—incites a fall,

It will end totally. If nothing on the wall,
Or in the locked safe; what's the point
Just a lot of hollow yesterdays—
Before more tomorrows.

For Trudy

Beyond the sashed window—
I found fabric violet edged
A sampler of cursive embroidery

I heard the sound of a homesick heart
Evoke each loss within its chambers
Or was it, pounding—the pounding
Of a woman kneading bread

There is a cat asleep on the summer bed
Violets and day lilies for eternity's vase
Beyond the window, honey-suckle vine
Over the high stone wall

Washing on the line like a flock of gulls
Ironing in the hall, crisp and white
Always carrying something in your hands
Brought us more love—untrammeled heart,

The one who grieved the ancestral land
The one who grieved her younger brother
Who was shot by enemy soldier,
The loved one, the younger, not much older

Tears tighten your eyes as days hurry by
What should I have said to you—
I watched you undoing knitting
Skeins of heather wool for the children

Even when your clothes worn thin
Scarce, elder-voice longed in the distance
Tell us to wrap well, stays with me
And with the apple blossom's confetti
A garden overgrown, violets' perfumery
Shares the same stillness.

FIRE AND SNOW

As winter leaves fell, blades on cold grass
Now there are, filthy clouds of hazardous orange
Scorching the skies, against the world's limits
Perhaps something sinister, re-inhaled with ash
Smoke and dust remain in our lungs
As black summer burning, returns to the heart
And this time, of stone, passes like slow hearse
procession
 Yet, here I am—star-spangled, gold-bangle woman
—a statistical survivor.

AT TRIAL BAY

Past the German Bridge,
a place they called the castle
all sorts of bondage of histories
there is a mapped out blue-print

final plan for internment blocks
the night is long on a single bed
even if any moment could speak
we would not understand

with black-castings under deadlock
come back and bar the door
a hallway of austere ventilation
with limited windows, iron bars

black lightening indecorous
and with some paint astray
like some thin skin, rotted and lost
I made a kind of mortmain pact

the lawsome that foils the visitor
night as long as ecclesiastical year
artists' painted through lost times

I almost heard your voice, in mine
when they gathered loose bones
there was silent truce amongst the past
we could guess the tenuous ghosts
all in an interminable year

you curse the hours of waking,
you do not wear your own clothing
sleep five minutes every twelve hours
all contempt for your oppressors.

ENDEAVOR

How many men have worn themselves thin
Wandering north or south, as months pass
Each place shows its crevasse and calamity

A mountain of ice, cold land retinue
Ice is worthless in an unscented world,
Snowstorm like a companion, disappearing off

They divined, with some of ice-men's wisdom
Once a year, they broke their way through
Leaning the crystal railing, sound as ice breaks

A strange place to promise away life, breathing
Chill air, as frozen mist thickened the season
What a place for the homeless to call home

Taking up temporary residence in mizzen huts
New ice still thin, ten thousand boot steps
Into whiteout conundrum, whatever blankness

Seabirds cleave cold clouds above
A blue-whale swims, prey in its mouth
Fish after fish darted into the sea; numberless

A fisherman's harpoon rusted by absence
And the backs of seals, glisten victorious
Echoes of seal and whales, dolorous

As man headed back through wild hum
Not having found the sled, winter to outrun
First tracks scud across snow, abominable

A wolf-skin hood with ice leaves jangling
Past his breath, a shivering cur mindless
Ashamed to look at his face against coldness

Frost-bite flowers on his cheeks, all of those
Teeth chattering from time to time,
Drifts of white snow masked his shoulders

Thick snow plastered on his broken coat
Everyone speaks well of the lost man
He found his dog pack, gathered them home

Cloistered to chains, slip away colder,
Timeless howling, makes long night, longer
But sound dies away, each passing floe.

ONE BLUE MOON

There is a circle marked on the floor
where feet are allowed no freedom
pacing the trackless cell, in his sadness

gaze toward the kempt garden
days when red flowers bloom
the gladioli cultivate one's mind

there is a corner of sky above
one's head, where thoughts hide
songbirds fly silently across
straying eagle on the way

stone wall by the blue sky
when one knocks on the door
no one left to answer

strange notes from gypsy violin
the moon in one's arms
it'll follow the prisoner unasked

to the end of the world
opiates of motherland, songs
said to be humanly tragic
a thousand hauteur of loss
each in its own way
                    can cause death—
past midnight, and you, *The One*
still haven't gone to sleep.

TRAVELS IN ANTARCTICA

One page of a letter from the explorer
Read from beginning to end, cold dregs
Through the eyes of someone left alone—
Monotonous thoughts on ice floe
Struggling with pure Whiteness

Layers of thought, lingering torpor
And that sound of fevered breath
I sustain all this underworld heat
I am cold, that I grow colder
I am old, that I grow older...

Wait for signs of saviors, no word comes
Snow whitens this old coat, cold metonymy
Ice mountains throw their majesties
More than thoughts could answer
In the coldest part of the world

Take the brass buttons from my coat
And give them to our children
Today and yesterday, I remember
You gave me the warmth enough
Feel your fingers, warm in the glove

Keeping me awake, as they would
Had I a remnant, you would keep
The ancient pulse of germ and birth
Belonged to you.

ANON

Where are the rich ones now?
Like the dust in the Florentine villa
Or argent's mirror, remnant of fate
Gold and fame's tempted ruin

It's difficult to paint the bones
At times, a moon hangs ominously
Trove of hesitant stars, on and on
Heavens never-ending compendium

Right and wrong, untold tome
It's difficult to carve a cherry-stone
A calabash more than rudimentary
Make tea, by red burning leaves

Ice and flowers, snow and tree
Wind and moon for company
It's difficult to paint the bones
Roses scattered in the neighborhood

Enough red petals for every bed
Beyond the pale moon's dust

Red sun slants westward
Morning soon is night
then, doors lock
—privacy?

OPIUM

The genesis of two traced back to this love affair
There were seeds in a mouth, from the first fig tree:
If love is a work of composition, you are the painter

If love is running its own course, I will swim the river
If love is the raw material from which I am shaped—
Look for me again Lover, I will carry your children

A boy child on my right hip and a girl on my left
You will find me again by my long hair—
You will see me in a dream.

THE VILLAGE YEAR

Walking together on the high road
Kindred steps, all leaden feet
Passive and tractable our footprints

Who laments the village has changed
Like fitting a glove, back on a hand
Or lay sadness, on the back of a moth

Disheveled in the wind, proof we are here
A hundred possibilities, fit-full and discursive
Snowy buds of roses in December, impatient

Thatched cottages latticed by ivy curtains
The village cricket-green peaceful on Sunday
Strong downward current, against the upstream

Like a breath you gasp, but can hold it less
Iridescent bubbles float on a foul stream
Mole-hill mountains imprisoned in winter

The earth and snow are glued together
Ravens cover their face with their wings

Because of saw and falling axe, hedgerow done
But centuries of doves kept their reverie
Passing the song's arch from season to season
A swallow heading south, the flood of air
Curling wreaths of clouds in the maelstrom.

COMPANION OF SOLITUDE

Name the man, The Prisoner—

As he, stenciling leaf-flower
of a patriarchal folk-blessing
closer to the vault of ceiling

like Sistine vault of Southern Stars
this angelic frieze of Prussian blue
like stray silk brushed against the wall

of dank cell, for the incarcerated one
all this paint, like a silent poem
and yet, he was thinking, another place

back home, summer in the village,
the hours of waking, he will obey
labor hard, breakwater, and old railway

black as a hearse, ink black horses,
black carriage, silk cord or shackles
has no beginning, middle or end

who is that man with feet bare
sits at night on the willow-back chair
leaves his clothes to dry them out

now, a scarecrow wears your coat
make-shift roost for passing crows
and gladioli you planted, red riot

outside the silent room's silence
it is easy to imagine the changeling
oak of Black Forest in shadow

blue whales' triumph in Trial Bay inlet
things that catch the prisoner's eye,
some proof, if they take away the sun and sky

and a man given a dark valedictory
two hundred years, we come back to hear
your voice, once more, in homeward garden.

Old Movies

A block of ice floats faster than a stone
The killer whale follows the seal
When wind is in the east

Then fishes bite the least
First you are carpenter of ice
Hearing the whole world splice

Wind is in the south
Blows bait in the fish's mouth
Wintertime with blood and brine

Rich fruit cake and potted ham
Bottled peach and pilchard can
Mules will carry your provisions

Marrowbones and lardy tins
Sou'wester from a whale foreskin
Boil tallow and fat will follow

Blow the wind loud and fast
It will lower at the final blast
The longest day and shortest night

Snuff out candle, shut the light
Preserves and wine outlive our marrow
Come when it will, it comes tomorrow

The raven with a sack-full of sorrow
The mast, gaff and the boom
Glaciers lay like grander ruins

All things eventually lose solid value
One's unlucky, two's lucky
Three's health, four's wealth

Five is weather thick and thin
Six seized flag with contraband stars
The cloth endures anything

When wind is in the west
Then fishes bite the best
Lose a minnow to catch a whale

Catch them on Sunday your safety seek
Storm shall have you rest of the week
Slip on the same ice, twice in old boots

During the curfew of pack-ice hum
Mules die, sled dogs succumb one by one
If you harpoon the fish, first shoot the whale

If you use a spear, use the longest rope
To capture a woman's heart, give her children
If a family, also limits, lissome words

Like the end of a never-ending conversation
Regret and sadness, our eulogies
Wasted last saliva on a postage stamp

Last letter back to the mainland
Thank you for your blackberry jam
Was never bitter and never sweet

Wife take care of our newborn
Look for nightshade in new wine
Children look after your mother

Walk fast in snow, in ice walk slow
In extremes of heat and cold
When ice and snow are both together

Sit by the burning log and save boot-leather
Books and friends should be few
Bread of pleasure, drink of measure

All sorts of perishables and survival rations
Rob royal bees and leave us honey-less
Empty hive and sweet impoverishing

Bones on the ice floe will quickly decay
White burns your eyes if you catch
The glaring cold, white riffled landscape

But if by chance, you return, this image
From a thousand-year journey, of buried dust
Returning home will be by accident

Or years spent wishful thinking, placed in memory
Still, as my life draws on, I light memory candles
So we find each other— in another dream

Beyond the ship of sailor boys
The night-man speaks to the night
Come out, all your black storms

The snow shall speak for the ice
Dark rum toddy says the sailor boy
Is drunk from a beaten cup
Your deeds earned crown nor wreath
Now the explorer's book is shut.

On Common Land

This was the world, all about was his,
An empty world, leaves no single trace

But for that, even then, it was illusion
A foreclosure sign tacked on oak tree

And whosoever should try to trespass,
If you know longer, know your heart,

I was a thought, part earth, part flower
Likely to be useful later, as past logic

Perhaps he was lord of the garden, also
From worms, to frogs, naturally enough

And to gardeners, cane chair, dirt plot
The gold-digger's undermining epic

Tomorrow, I'll go to the auction room
To settle a lynch pin of resentment.

SILVER SPOON

If nothing is meant to be simple,
The house may be small, keep it sublime

Repair the clock face, keeps better time
Begs to be a kept, the wedding date set

On the anniversary of the adversaries
Fateful as a starry night in Verona

Every opera sang itself, beyond blue
Pearl necklace, gold watch, solitaire ring

Encircles the silvered mirror of another
Affair of the heart, as the money goes

Pay a man to prune a rose
Get a dog, but the dog gets lost

Windows or rooms—lock in frost
Familiar with the cradle, what matters this,
That willful error why it is said,
If there is a gap in the soul,
The devil inside, never fully lets you go.

THE MILL-HOUSE

In his Lordship's garden ambiguous
A man stood indifferently,
In whose house, more was the pity

The children were real, not Arcadian
A perch for young sparrows, this old garden,
Already level with weeds,

Then you came here to add a heart of stone
In whose little garden, all shall see
The water clock drips on—

                      snow the old man is gone

So, she became *The Gardener*
An old woman swallows a stone of a tree
Now, an orchard grows inside her

Forfeit true smile with a thought
Even as leaves fall from apple tree,
One single leaf, retains ardency.

CANDLE IN THE MIRROR

I keep changing countries,
like counterfeit money,
hurrying on, afraid to look back,

like a phantom dividing in two
like a candle between mirrors
sailing into the sun.

I ache when you are sad, she said
but when from a long distant past
...nothing subsists,

after the people have gone,
after the things broken scatter,
taste and smell alone,

more fragile, more immaterial,
more persistent, more fruitful,
remain there for a long time,

like souls remembering,
waiting in the ruins of it all,
in a simple drop of ink,

there is no scent to remember
a man she has never touched
in a tiny drop…begins
recollections write themselves.

THE DESERT

Once, upon another time—Us
where one stood in sun, the other in shade
in the shadows of each other, I followed you

not knowing where we would end, until
you reached a place of fabled cartography
where men perish, and when I looked

in the direction of the horizon, I saw
nothing more, ahead but sea of sand,
this inertia extending as far

as my eye could reach, on one side
sand, formed hills like waves,
your body lashed into that position

by storms; on the other side
like the waters of a still lake,
rippled by wind. I was frightened

that is why I left in a hurry.
I thought I would rather risk death
from destruction by some fever wind,

or starvation, rather than stay
behind with you, to leave this place
for good, will crush the faint-hearted
but survivors manage to: live-on
the dead are gone forever
in an after-life, who can-ever imagine?

DIARY OF LOST MAN

Autumn
'Grass etches the soles of my feet;
I walk the tract of land reclaimed from the harbor,
sand slowly drying out, until the fallen
buildings rise again—the jail is in my heart.'

Winter
'Snow is all around, befalls blanket of cold comfort,
symbol of inexplicable hardship borne of the chaos,
envelops in dead of winter, like the hand of god,
gravity holds me together: I return to the earth
and water from where I came, once second,
so eager, little did I know of fate, little believing
certain failure to survive, possible, only question is,
why did I fail?'

Spring
'Life and this world part company on a hard schedule,
mercifully unknown. I have no life plan, no map
to circumvent its torments, as the endless uncertainty
gradually becomes more trying than the final event,
yet I cling to a hope of personal infinity, made

possible by missing the surety of life's exact
dimensions; the desperate desolate prayer somehow
overwrites my reason.'

Summer

'Nothing of value, no good and noble work
will stay or slow this vengeance. I should spare you
these thoughts, but to do so would spare you from
myself and I am incapable. I do know that I wish you
better, that I wish you the facility to rise above these
convulsive and crippling truths, to rise above this
and all other impediments to a happy life. You say,
'Life is but a dream'. So, we keep on dreaming.'

THE LATE SALESMAN

I am going to a Seaside town,
an old fishing village,
un-selfconscious and *un-urban*,

she said, what I would give
just to eat wild salted whelk
with a fork, or bent safety-pin

back from making the world safe,
for another unneeded shopping center
Pittsburgh is the pits, bleak, bare—
beyond a city's redemption

I've been going there for thirty-five years
and never seen the sun shine.
the road to the airport under construction
for the length of my lifetime

so far, and yet, this city is consistently rated
as one of the "most livable" in the country
this is how you live life—go figure!

CONFESSION

Just older than a girl, seventeen
Brought him a rose, for these memories

A bedspread on a virgin's bed,
White sweat beneath crewel branches,

Silk figures stand guard outside pagodas
Trailing tendrils and tiny leaves

Embroidered birds of paradise hover
Mimosa outlined by pearls

As seeds spill on the tree pattern
Masked the flowers, covered wild fruits

Linen thread on raw silk taints
Delicate dewberry butterflies

Caught up in beggars velvet
As if skin is the last to feel

Who draws the libidinous quilt
This body lost its original outline

In this alchemy between lovers
Who forgets the taste of violets in a mouth?
When you turn away this heart
And everything you touch unravels.

ALVESTON MANOR

We remember familiar sounds of the countryside
Following the crows, dark upon some wizard way
The sky deepens like a scarlet poppy burnt
It had a time, and is another—a pall creeps upward

Here in the windless orchard, ghosts are gathering
Leaving them cold, flock of geese, lord of the manor
Gamekeeper, arborist, mistress, cadence of history
Or daughter of the King, just older than a girl,

Brook House tenants are ghosts on the register
Ancestor of his, was granted the dynasty of kings
Son of Adam, sold the manor to Robert,
Land dispute with Apple-Bee, whoever paid tax

Of the honey-bees, or the honey-comb—
Knew the daughter of the King, older than a girl,
Something sweet seemed to cling around her,
Some shapes breathed on a mirror, and melting away.

GIVE OR TAKE

Militia money is buried under the stairs
By the wife of a serving militia man

Gold buried above, silver below ground
A life, a presence, like a lightening-phrase

A list of unread letters, shook out truth
The pen parched by long disuse

Conflicted histories, an old rubbish-heap
But the memory; a well-ordered cupboard

Paid for providing lodging for homeless
The dislocated slip back into place

Paid for window broken by stone
Resolution for deserted home

Paid for rustic salves of salvation
Clear-cut as a sculptor's thought

Paid the artist for the portrait
A ruby like a drop of blood

Paid for the streetwalker
Rules like dresses, set aside

Paid for close shave with profanity
A thought, like cold worm in a mind

Provided beasts of farm and burden
Some green field with a touch of rain

Conjuring, an animal out of the dark
Knife-cut across the sinews

Built a shelter for lost black dog
Visits those forlorn eyes

Supplied enameled clock face
Unconscious as cast-away hour

Supplied wormwood in sugar glass
Easy as a poet's dream

Gave money to fishes school
All sounds lost in woodland river

Gave legacy to the cloud tamer
A whistle of air, the flight of arrows

Worked on smiles of forgotten saints
As silent as the sheeted dead

Provided matches ever-lasting bonfire
An incessant play of fireworks

An impudent trick, this hackneyed
Anxiety with its unwelcome mazes

Paid for a road to the feather pit
Cedar white with the hoar frost

Paid for mending angelic realms
A bird on an out-worn cage
Vibration of a song, rings true gold
Voices of the women when they sang together.

STRATFORD-UPON-AVON

There is a post office on White Horse Hill
Fern Bank House, a grocer's store
One butcher delivers on Fridays

Probable son of Richard
Owned Shakespeare's dwelling
In Pigeon Green, birds over field
The stacks of corn in gold array

Mother of Leyton's child
Paid to wash John Reeves sheet
Has a child to Thomas,
Echo of a natal dream

Friendship with Lady Coventry
Who brought him a rose,
Dew on the sleeping flower
Take her hand in marriage

Had a child to Mary Lock,
Widow, tailor, surveyor
Footsteps treading on wool,

Dim scent of violets
Daughter of the leather stall owner
Saddler, then shoe repairer
Lame shoemaker sold her store
Sense and thought gone, fled

Father of Susannah's child
Receives fee for marrying
Taught Shakespeare's father
Night thought threads a dream

Referee for apple-bee dispute
And as for Shakespeare's debt
Paid for straw and rods
To thatch the leaky roof

Mice steal in and out, fear of light
Cleared Ivy Close and Church Hill
Tattered effigy in the wheat field
Cleared Red Hill plantation

Vaporous shapes half seen
And the blue blood between
Cleared Luscombe Wood
Wind faint, in cold grass
Cleared the last remaining Common
Now great black ravens haunt the woods.

HALLOW HALL

In the empty house when no human presence
For centuries, the child's voice, like a bird call
Haunted perfume of pressed flowers
As whole house spread with hope

Candlelight like beaten moonbeams
Thunder-clouds held in chamois air
Winter sky grows cold after sunset
White moon shares ancient sorrows

Snow fell, in landscape of dream,
Draws genii from foundation
Obstinate rolls over the heavy sleeper
After he is called to get up

Bell rung far down, hums the water
Veiled ghosts hurry past, land of shadows
Glitter, forked flash of lightening
Rattles windows, sharp and brilliant

Finger of clock, her shadow came
Streams over memory like a forest flame
Blown moths against rose-white cloth
Vanish like phantasmagoria.

BLACK BOOK

Creaking doors ajar
Creeping rust insidious
Mind's an open fire
Direct and instant
House damaged by fire
Itemize funeral costs
Infirm, old man—
Still as stone
Vast blank linen
Widow of Henry,
Dies six weeks later
Lost to us, mines of gold
Silent and cold
Through moonlight trees,
Quiet ghosts sound
Haunting the village,
Wine flows like blood—
Ran legend of hidden treasure
Flew raven for good measure.

QUIETER HISTORIES

Here, private recollections and village histories re-
begin
Charity for charities sake, an alias bequeaths four
wagons
Distributing coal for bonfire, reference to poison
mushrooms

Woodcarver, maker of hoops and hurdles, made a
church bell
Street cleaner buys a manor house, lets someone else
sweep up
Rob, the tailor, was nicknamed Dandy Patch,

Disputes with John of Daisy Hill, his boy killed by a
horse
Takes in six child evacuees, act of enclosure war's
allocation
Now and forever lord of the manor, builds us a 12th
century church.

Whosoever lived at Park House. Died at Park House.
Poet, friend of Jago, Godfather to his son
Curate to the ferryman or fisherman
Poet, vicar, a summary of quieter histories

Blacksmith, son of Fred, father one winter
Has a child, vagrant, no longer heard of

Held an allotment of livestock. Entrant in greased pig
chase
House damaged by storm. One charity school in the
churchyard
Bakery delivered by donkey. Motherless, sent to
orphan school
In all of this, who was as witness
to a drowning?

THE CITY

Walked across the harbor bridge
Returned after ribbon was cut
We ended up in the city
And our distance recorded
By strumpets and harlots,
By the heart of the city,
By the golden milestone
All lives are recorded
There is a door with a lock
A bonfire in the back yard
Shadows over the negatives
Once the luck falls the other way,
Reduces the list to three
Wait. Go. Stay.

THE ROOM

Wild flowers on Venetian wall—
canvas tent, palace, grass shack
rooms remember us, like that
it has always been there
as a room to be entered
I have looked the other way
closed the door
swallowed the key
but the door is open
I am lying on the bed
I have been here waiting for you
a thousand-thread count sheets—
find me in the unfolding
we were never weighted down
warm stones of our breathing
we build a castle with our bodies
I know the faraway corners
more of you—skin-tight secrets
my lips say the password
it was not our hotel—
we were both visitors.

THE SIGNATURE

To step back in the before—

I have stood here for ages
books strewn about the room

get used to the red carpet
curve of the balustrade

in the Hotel of Fortitude
its many mirrored doors

like all remembered things
I have regrets locked in them

we left, so we could return
let the world be the world

a handshake for believers
until the plague was over

first, they sent dreams,
then illusions; share with us

there will be more money
in your shallow pockets

fool, to put your faith
in absolute liars

whose ulterior motive
the dark and darker

whether you say yes, or no
the best dream is broken

worse than any bone
so, I took back the dream

no longer believe in dreamers'
whether you are a hoarder,

or a giver—if you are poorer
or richer, long thoughts

all things change in the mind
if you force a signature
the right way, or what is left
it will be money, coming

there are bonds and deeds
there are crooked nooks

red book in the rusted safe
money under the mattress

gold buried in the garden
grand nugget as big as my hand

a diamond large as a fist
pearl-earring thrown into the sea

when the mighty, don't trust
we might better be poor

we might better be rich
homecoming on my mind

no further steps, please
a wrought iron wreath

and roof finial gone
a sense of thunder comes.

TRACES

What does it matter
put on a felt fedora or beret
if the caviar is chilled,
or the spoon mother-of-pearl
if the champagne is cold
there's a first-class ticket
there's a winning number
there's a seat allocation
everything is freedom
there's another way out
behind magician curtain
come in, sit down
but the planes are grounded
a desert in the jet-stream
planes with wings of cloth
a wooden war propeller
gathers dust in the attic
hell, take the last ticket
until the plague is over
we'll wait for the world.

PRELUDE

If she happens into the attic room—
Windows open to the sea
Old volcano in its dormancy
Glass syringe boils in the pot

But now, *The Traveler* tips powder
In the jade-stone dish,
A drop or two of water, mercurial
Earth and river, to write a poem

But I have no pocket to hold your poem
Or, a map of where we are going,
Or, history of where we have come from.

LITMUS

The sun has set, the moon ahead
slow, wet nights before us
a night of shot down stars
pass into a nightmare
read judgment pages
over again in pale light
fate, outcast strangers
like floating a paper boat
down the gutter, in a flood
net of rain carelessly spread
in a raft of bittered lead
now, fat years are over
to fall out of favor
here where you and I
no difference is there
in the city of canvas tents
or learn to live without
with a last match
we strike into the wind
to get used to the dark
thought that this will never end
but now I know, compassion,

that is the way of you—
you always gave me rice to eat
simply put—white pinions in a bowl.

THE CULVERT

Most nights, there is a wolf-wind
Shakes weatherboard houses
Shows its teeth in shifting moods
Rank and position unchallenged

And know, there was a small child
Like straw in a gust of wind
Hiding from the wolf's eye
At the farthest edge of sleep

Reckless impulse of supremacy
Touches of private composure
Light gossip and wild luxuriance
In quiet and lonely home
Near the presence of wild distaste
Visits of angels, few and far between.

EPIC OF MIND

Like separated siblings—we are
Kindred blood mingled into one
Born onward by deed of ignorance
Until buried hopes rise up

The sentries come and go
By a curious reprieve of fate
There were happy turns of thought
Forged fiction with young minds

Conjuring commensurate holidays
Conscious of so-called nest
Stratagem of fake inheritance
Days of a rankling misfits

Throngs of serious monotony
Disguise the silent suspicion
Stung by the other thought
Dreams and visions take a turn

Yes, The *Master of Fate* is unscrupulous.
And know, that in the midnight garden
Even earth's decaying leaves

Footsteps upon wool, I am sure
Echo from some antenatal dream

A sparrow pecked off all the gold buttons
From Grandmother's only winter coat
—gave all her treasures to the children,
like a world of sunshine.

If Astrid

She made of stars
Orion, Sirius, shining
And the world, became diamond

The moon followed her home
She lived in a canvas tent
Outside the house, with a stray cat

The grass was an outspread mat
She strung common white daisies
To made a necklace of summer

Now she looks in the mirror,
Hair white as pale jade
And enmity with that
Not young, but not yet old
The girl is the woman
Remember her?

FOR MARIA

It was a year of plague
A breath under a mask
Like a flag on the face
Confused mass of expressions
Sudden gust of infected air
Returns like thistledown
New variant mutant strains
Like a pointing finger
Handshake cold as death
Keep borders locked down,
Torments us like a list of dying
Gift cards and mail order, anything
For a well-ordered cupboard
Notable faces on computer screen
Like a bookshelf of thought
Drinking coffee on the café balcony
Maintaining social distance
Shadows upon shadow
Days ordinary as a cup of coffee
Like a gold-caged bird
In case of a change in thought,
A tune that everyone knows

To write a note to leave behind
Wild as chaos, like winter weather
All silent as sheeted dead
Include a recipe for mango chutney
Unconscious as a wooden spoon
At full tide, people swam in the estuary

Coat pockets weighted down—
with memories and river stones.

COMPARED

Invitation to Sapphire Beach
Indifferent as a tourist

Everything would collapse
As if by enchantment

Fish heads in deep trash
Overwhelm the horizon

Cucumbers on the vine
Green masses tangled

Passion fruit over the coup
Unconscious of honey bees

Holy basil all bitter-sweet
As perfume stretched away

Parsley gone to late seed
Outlooking summer breeze

Unnamed flowers in garden
Cleave path unkempt grasses

A strong smell of citronella
Dominant as a yellow sun

A wide mouthed owl
Feathers the grey sky
Motionless, still, sentinel
Like a passing thought
Remembered out—
conjuring the rabbit.

Twenty-First Century

Five lottery tickets, almost won
Luck sets its own chagrin
Random numbers intangible

Dumb as fishes in dry bowl
The champagne bottle emptied

 Books delivered in a blizzard
A measurable sadness opposes

Arbitrary money in the bank
Letter, after, letter, overtaken

Austerity in a downtown shelter
One breaks loose and goes

Coldest evening wavers record
Vibration of snow fallen too fast

Easy to ask private questions
Quiet recluse in a crowd

As simple as Sunday morning
Slow shadows still as a stone

Clothing left in the dryer
Avalanche of white sheets

Doves in the winter garden
Call out, same fluent song
Middle notes of coronet bells
Soft as a flake of snow on her cheek.

THE ENVOI

I have been on the island twenty years
In the end, I cannot stay
The canoe coming to take me
The women in bright clothes
Gather on the long pier
In the end, I cannot stay

Everyone has a white flower
Behind their ear, you appear
The canoe coming to take me
Mamma has given me one
And then there is none
The canoe coming to take me

White tiare flower over the right ear
Looking for a lover, more or less
Stay, she whispers, and undresses
Tonight, we put scarlet flowers in our hair
And go looking for one another
Swim in the lagoon, in moonlight
I have a million things to tell you—*but not now*
In the end, I cannot stay,
The canoe coming to take me.

SUSAN BLANSHARD

Poet Susan Blanshard was born in Hampshire, England. She is a poet, essayist, best-selling author, revisionist poetry editor and literary critic. Her nomadic childhood and multicultural past color her writing. Susan has published selected poems such as *'Fragments of the Human Heart'*, *'Poems from the Alley,'* *'Quieter Histories: Winter to Winter.'* *'Send the Raven'*, and full-length books in poetic prose include *'Sheetstone'*, Spuyten Duyvil, New York and *'Honey in the Blood'*, *'Sleeping With The Artist'*, Page Addie Press, United Kingdom. Her selected poetry and essays are published in numerous international literary magazines including 'The World's Literary Magazine Projected Letters', 'Six Bricks Press', 'Lotus International Women's Magazine', 'ICORN International Cities of Refuge'. 'PEN International

Women Writers' Magazine. PEN International Writers Committee The Fourth Anthology, Our Voice', 'Coldnoon International Journal of Travel and Literature'.

Susan Blanshard is the English Poetry Stylist and Editor for seventeen translated works: poetry, literature, literary critiques, and short stories, including the book winner of the 10th Cikada Prize, Sweden.